# Summer Study

## For the Child Going into Second Grade

Written by **Christine Hood**

Illustrations by **Hector Borlasca**

**FlashKids**

New York

New York

An Imprint of Sterling Publishing
387 Park Avenue South
New York, NY 10016

ISBN 978-1-4114-6547-3

Distributed in Canada by Sterling Publishing
c/o Canadian Manda Group, 165 Dufferin Street
Toronto, Ontario, Canada M6K 3H6
Distributed in the United Kingdom by GMC Distribution Services
Castle Place, 166 High Street, Lewes, East Sussex, England BN7 1XU
Distributed in Australia by Capricorn Link (Australia) Pty. Ltd.
P.O. Box 704, Windsor, NSW 2756, Australia

For information about custom editions, special sales, and premium and corporate purchases, please
contact Sterling Special Sales at 800-805-5489 or specialsales@sterlingpublishing.com.

Manufactured in Canada
Lot #:
6  8  10  11  9  7
03/14

www.flashkids.com

Cover design and production by Mada Design, Inc.

# DEAR PARENT,

Your child is out of school for the summer, but this doesn't mean that learning has to stop! In fact, reinforcing academic skills in the summer months will help your child succeed during the next school year. This Summer Skills workbook provides activities to keep your child engaged in all the subject areas—Language Arts, Math, Social Studies, and Science—during the summer months. The activities increase in difficulty as the book progresses by reviewing what your child learned in first grade and then introducing skills for second grade. This will help build your child's confidence and help him or her get excited for the new school year!

As you and your child go through the book, look for "Fast Fact" or "On Your Own" features that build upon the theme or the activity on each page. At the back of this book you'll find a comprehensive reading list. Keep your child interested in reading by providing some or all of the books on the list for your child to read. You will also find a list of suggested summer projects at the back of this book. These are fun activities for you and your child to complete together. Use all of these special features to continue exploring and learning about different concepts all summer long!

As your child completes the activities in this book, shower him or her with encouragement and praise. You can feel good knowing that you are taking an active and important role in your child's education. Helping your child complete the activities in this book provides him or her with an excellent example—that you value learning, every day! Have a wonderful summer, and most of all, have fun learning together!

# TABLE OF CONTENTS

 # HIKING TRAILS

The numbers on each path follow a pattern. Write numbers on the lines to complete each path. Then write the pattern. The first one is done for you.

1.  **2  4  6  8  10  12  14  16  18  20**

    Pattern: __+2__

2.  **2  3  4  5  6  7  8  9  10  11  12**

    Pattern: __+1__

3.  **3  6  9  12  15  18  21  24  27  23**

    Pattern: __+3__

4.  **5  10  15  20  25  30  35  40  45**

    Pattern: __4__

## FAST FACT
Did you know that some pine trees live to be 2,000 years old? Some of these trees grow to more than 300 feet tall. That's taller than a 20-story building!

# MORE OR LESS?

Write **more** or **less** on the line to complete each sentence.

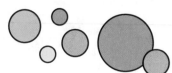

**1.** A ride on the Ferris wheel costs _____less_____ than a pony ride.

**2.** A pig weighs _____ than a goldfish.

**3.** A hot dog costs _____ than cotton candy.

**4.** A bag of popcorn weighs

_____ than a stuffed animal.

**5.** A balloon costs _____

than a funny hat.

**6.** An apple pie weighs

_____ than a cookie.

## ON YOUR OWN
Have you ever been to a fair or carnival? Write a short story about it.

# FALLING LEAVES

Add the numbers on each leaf. Color the leaves with matching sums the same color.

1.  3
    +7

2.  2
    +6

3.  9
    +3

4.  6
    +6

5.  7
    +4

6.  2
    +8

7.  5
    +6

8.  10
    +5

9.  7
    +8

10. 4
    +4

11. 5
    +4

12. 8
    +1

8

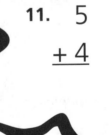

# BUILDING WORDS

Below are the mixed-up letters of a word. How many little words can you make from the letters? Can you find the big word?

o r h m e t

**1.** Words with 2 letters:

_____
_____
_____
_____

**2.** Words with 3 letters:

_____
_____
_____
_____
_____
_____

**3.** Words with 4 letters:

_____
_____
_____
_____
_____

**4.** Word with 5 letters:

_____

**5.** Word with 6 letters (the big word):

_____

## ON YOUR OWN
How many words can you make from the letters of your name? Write your name on a piece of paper. Then see how many words you can make from the letters.

9

An **adjective** describes a person, place, or thing. Circle the adjectives in each sentence.

1. Lisa's (white) puppy played in the (muddy) puddle.

2. The tiny mouse ate bits of yellow cheese.

3. The large zoo was full of noisy animals.

4. Her short hair was curly and soft.

5. Mia took a long nap under the shady tree.

6. The crisp apple tasted sweet.

7. My new teacher gave us tasty cupcakes.

8. Tennis is a fun game to play on a warm day.

9. My friend Carlos is smart and funny.

10. Jess ate a slice of spicy, hot pizza.

**ON YOUR OWN**
Look in the mirror. Write at least five adjectives describing what you see.

 # IN THE BEGINNING

Write the beginning letters **ch** or **sh** to complete each word.

**1.**

_ch_ air

**2.**

_____ eep

**3.**

_____ oe

**4.**

_____ ell

**5.**

_____ eese

**6.**

_____ icken

**7.**

_____ ild

**8.**

_____ ip

**ON YOUR OWN**
Take a walk around your neighborhood. How many things do you see that begin with the letters **ch** or **sh**? Make a list!

# HEALTHFUL HABITS

Some activities will keep you healthy. Color the pictures that show children doing healthy activities.

# MY FAMILY

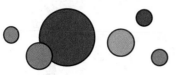

Who are the people in your family? Do you know your grandparents' names?
Do you have brothers or sisters? With a parent's help, fill in this family tree.

Mother's Side

Father's Side

_____ and _____
Grandfather            Grandmother

_____ and _____
Grandfather            Grandmother

_____
Mother

_____
Father

My Brothers and Sisters

_____        _____

_____        _____

_____
ME!

Family Tree

## ON YOUR OWN

Who are you most like in your family? Draw a picture of yourself with this relative. Write a few words telling how you are alike.

# FIND THE NUMBER WORDS

Find and circle the number words for **1** to **12** in the word search. Words can go across or down.

| one | two | three | four | five | six |
|-----|-----|-------|------|------|-----|
| seven | eight | nine | ten | eleven | twelve |

| A | B | H | Y | J | K | M | L | T | D |
|---|---|---|---|---|---|---|---|---|---|
| O | N | E | J | N | T | F | C | W | N |
| Y | V | F | S | P | Q | S | X | E | A |
| G | E | I | G | H | T | I | U | L | S |
| W | S | V | B | Y | C | X | X | V | E |
| H | B | E | T | H | R | E | E | E | V |
| T | E | N | M | Y | T | Z | S | T | E |
| H | B | G | F | O | U | R | G | W | N |
| M | N | N | I | N | E | M | E | O | A |
| E | L | E | V | E | N | H | N | Y | B |

**ON YOUR OWN**
Think of things that come in twos, threes, and fours. Make a list. For example: two eyes, three triplets, and four dog legs.

# SUBTRACTION ACTION

There are 10 subtraction problems in this puzzle. Each problem can go down or across. Circle each problem.

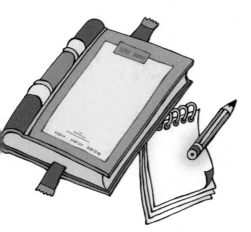

**Here is an example.**

| 11 | 5 | 7 |
|----|----|----|
| 6  | 4  | 2 |
| 10 | 1  | 8 |

| 12 | 15 | 13 | 5  | 11 |
|----|----|----|----|----|
| 6  | 10 | 8  | 2  | 6  |
| 6  | 3  | 5  | 4  | 5  |
| 3  | 7  | 2  | 5  | 12 |
| 3  | 0  | 3  | 10 | 7  |

**ON YOUR OWN**

Make your own subtraction puzzle for a friend to solve!

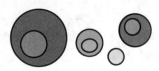  

# MAKING HALVES

When you divide something in half, you divide it into two equal parts. Color one-half of each group of objects.

**1.**

**2.**

**3.**

**4.**

**5.**

**6.**

## ON YOUR OWN

Count out different objects, such as candies, cookies, or buttons, in groups of 2, 4, 6, 8, and 10. Practice dividing each group in half.

# ACTION WORDS

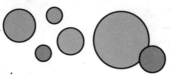

A **verb** is an action word. It tells what a person or object is doing. Circle the verbs in this paragraph.

Last week, I (got) a puppy. He has floppy ears and big brown eyes. He barks at the cat. He also chases butterflies and bees in the backyard. We walk to the park on Saturdays and play together. He is very friendly. Everyone loves him! I showed him how to jump in the air and catch balls. We go everywhere together. He is a good friend, so I named him Buddy. He comes whenever I call him by his name!

1. How many verbs are there? _____

Now, fill in the blanks with your own action words.

2. The lizard _____ up the wall.

3. My cat _____ in the sun.

4. The red car _____ down the street.

5. A snake _____ in the jungle.

6. I love to _____ in the sun.

## ON YOUR OWN

Go to a park or beach where there are a lot of people. What do you see happening? What are people doing? Write down all the action words you see.

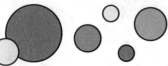
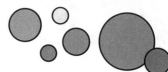

# NIFTY NOUNS

A **noun** is a person, place, or thing. Circle the noun in each row.

1. under     jump     (sock)     happy

2. kitten     sing     walk     pink

3. hear     swim     tiny     apple

4. loud     baby     blue     fluffy

5. child     fun     windy     sleep

6. drive     cold     beach     stop

7. silly     eat     milk     talk

8. dinosaur     over     pretty     skip

9. brown     sour     tasty     zoo

10. tall     open     home     ran

## FAST FACT

**Proper nouns** are the official names of people, places, and things. For example, **Abraham Lincoln**, **Mexico**, and **January** are all proper nouns.

Finish writing the name of each picture. Then draw a line between each pair of rhyming words.

1. c _____

2. m _____

3. b _____

4. b _____

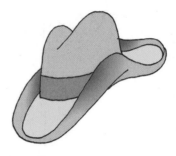

5. h _____

6. b _____

7. g _____

8. t _____

**ON YOUR OWN**
Write a sentence using each pair of rhyming words. For example: **The cat slept in the hat.**

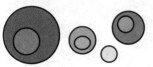 

Do you know all the parts of a plant? Label each part using the words in the box. Then color the picture.

stem

flower

seedling

leaf

roots

flower

## ON YOUR OWN

Go to a garden or flower store with a parent. See how many flowers you know by name. Carefully look at, touch, and smell the flowers. How many different colors and smells do you notice?

# WHERE DOES IT COME FROM?

Everything we eat, use, or wear comes from somewhere. Some things are made and then sold in markets. Some things come from plants and animals. Draw a line matching each object to the place it came from.

# FINISH THE PATTERN

Look at each row of numbers. Can you see a pattern? Finish each pattern. Then write the pattern.

**1.**   2   5   8   11   _14_   _17_   _20_

Pattern: _+3_

**2.**   1   5   9   13   _____   _____   _____

Pattern: _____

**3.**   14   12   _____   8   _____   _____   2

Pattern: _____

**4.**   3   6   9   _____   15   _____   _____

Pattern: _____

**5.**   10   9   8   _____   _____   _____   4   _____

Pattern: _____

**6.**   10   15   20   _____   30   _____   _____

Pattern: _____

**ON YOUR OWN**

Look at the clothes in your closet. Do you see patterns there? You might see stripes, polka dots, and other designs. Draw pictures of all the patterns you see.

# EARLY OR LATE?

Look at the time on each clock. Then circle **early** or **late** to finish each sentence.

**1.**

School starts at 8:00.
Jesse is (early) late.

**2.**

Soccer practice is at 3:45.
Mia is **early late**.

**3.**

The dog is walked at 10:30.
McKenzie is **early late**.

**4.**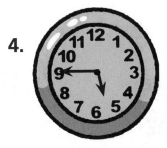

Dinner is at 6:00.
Devon is **early late**.

**5.**

Dance class begins at noon.
Keisha is **early late**.

**6.**

The picnic is at 2:15.
Noah is **early late**.

## ON YOUR OWN

For what activities do you have to be on time? Write a schedule for the times you have to be at school, lunch, soccer games, and other activities. Keep the schedule with you so you will know to be on time!

# WEIGH IT!

Look at each picture. Which unit of measure would you use? Circle **ounces** or **pounds**.

**1.**

(ounces)    pounds

**2.**

ounces    pounds

**3.**

ounces    pounds

**4.**

ounces    pounds

**5.**

ounces    pounds

**6.**

ounces    pounds

### ON YOUR OWN

Look at different objects around your house, such as a toothbrush, a spoon, a couch, and a television. Would you use **ounces** or **pounds**? Write the words ounces and pounds on several index cards. Then tape the index cards to the appropriate objects.

**7.**

ounces    pounds

**8.**

ounces    pounds

# AT THE END

Look at each picture. Say its name aloud. Then circle the word in each row with the same ending sound.

**1.** 　　wish　　　stop　　　(match)　　　lock

**2.** 　　star　　　bath　　　beach　　　bell

**3.** 　　wash　　　catch　　　boot　　　glass

**4.** 　　laugh　　　tax　　　pink　　　radish

**5.** 　　rug　　　pack　　　cent　　　jar

**6.** 　　sky
　　　　　　　　　finish
　　　　　　　　　cart
　　　　　　　　　hear

## ON YOUR OWN

Play a game with ending sounds in your own home. Pick objects from every room, such as **toy** and **bed**. Write down their names. Then think of words with the same ending sounds.

25

# WINDY WORDS

Write the best word to complete each sentence.
Use words from the word box.

| branch | school | day | lights | spooky |
|--------|--------|-----|--------|--------|
| dinner | bed | story | papers | hair |
| | fell | friend | shook | |

Today was a very windy ___day___! On my way to

_____, my hat blew down the street. My _____

was a mess! At school, I dropped my notebook and _____

went flying everywhere. My best _____ Joshua helped me catch

them. When I got home, a _____ had blown off of our tree.

It _____ in the yard. When the _____ went out,

we had to use candles to see. It was fun to eat _____ with

candles. Later, Dad told us a scary _____. Then, when I

was in _____, the wind_____ the windows.

It was _____!

Now, draw a picture of a windy day in the box.

 # TWO WORDS IN ONE

A **compound word** is a word formed by combining two words. To make compound words below, write the word for each picture. Then draw a line from the word to another word on the right. These two words will make a compound word!

 1. ___bird___                    ball

 2. _____                 fish

 3. _____                 bow

4. _____                 house

 5. _____                 bell

 6. _____                 shine

 7. _____                 cake

 8. _____                 place

Write the compound words below.

1. ___birdhouse___           2. _____

3. _____           4. _____

5. _____           6. _____

7. _____           8. _____

**ON YOUR OWN**
See how many compound words can you make with the word **some**.

27

# SOLID, LIQUID, GAS

Matter comes in three different states. The states are **solid**, **liquid**, and **gas**. Water can be all three states: ice, water, and steam. Label each picture below as a **solid**, **liquid**, or **gas**.

ice

water

steam

_____      _____      _____

Write **solid**, **liquid**, or **gas** after each word to tell what it is.

**1.** milk     liquid _____

**2.** rock     _____

**3.** air     _____

**4.** clay     _____

**5.** honey     _____

**6.** oil     _____

**7.** steam     _____

**8.** baseball     _____

**9.** book     _____

**10.** juice     _____

## ON YOUR OWN

Look in your refrigerator.
How many solids do you see?
How many liquids do you see?
Now look in your freezer.
Do you see any gases?

# USING A MAP

Maps help us get from one place to another. Look at the map below.
Then answer the questions.

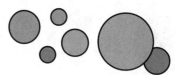

**ON YOUR OWN**
Draw a map of your bedroom. Pretend you are above looking down on it. Draw your bed, dresser, toys, and anything else you wish.

1. Which way would you turn on Elm Street to get to the post office? _right_

2. Which way would you turn on 1st Street to get to the park? _____

3. What street should you cross to get to the school?

_____

4. Are you closer to the park or the mountains? _____

5. The post office is on the corner of which two streets?

_____

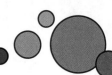

# HOW MANY INCHES?

You'll need a ruler for this activity. Use it to measure each object.

**1.** 2 inches

**2.** _____

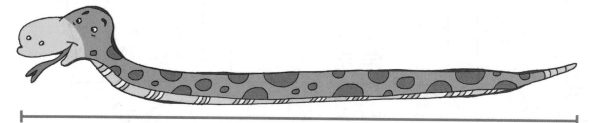

**3.** _____

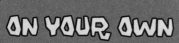

**ON YOUR OWN**

Use a ruler to measure items around your house. Measure your arm, a book, a plate, a toy, or even your cat's tail!

**4.** _____     **5.** _____

# EXACTLY THE SAME

Many things in nature have symmetry. **Symmetry** means that both sides are exactly the same. Draw the other half of this butterfly. Try to make it look exactly like the first half. Then color the butterfly.

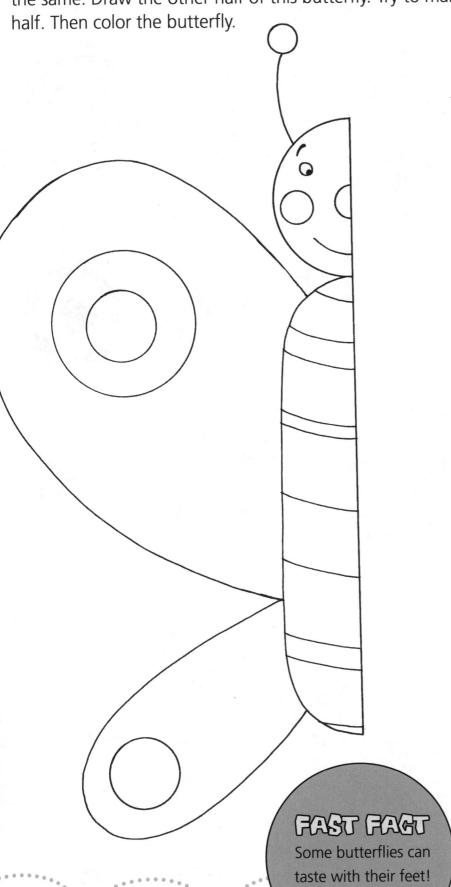

**FAST FACT**

Some butterflies can taste with their feet!

# WHAT DOESN'T BELONG?

Look at each row of objects. Circle the object in each group that doesn't belong. Then color the objects that belong.

**1.**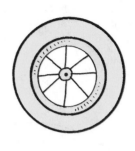

**2.**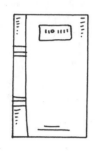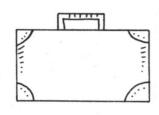

**3.**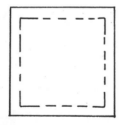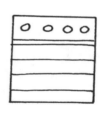

### ON YOUR OWN
Look for shapes around your house. What is round, like a ball? What is square, like a television? What is rectangular, like a bed?

**4.**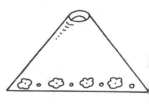

# SUNNY WORDS

Many things are organized in **alphabetical order**. This means they are arranged in order from **A** to **Z**, like words in a dictionary and names in a phone book. Rewrite each set of words in alphabetical order.

tiger
baboon
giraffe
lion

chair
dresser
bed
table

lunch
dinner
breakfast
snack

desk
pencil
book
student

**1.**
baboon
giraffe
lion
tiger

**2.**

**3.**

**4.**

summer
winter
fall
autumn

beach
park
zoo
mall

starfish
crab
whale
lobster

puppy
kitten
goldfish
mouse

**5.**

**6.**

**7.**

**8.**

## FAST FACT
The Sun is so bright because it is very hot. The Sun is 27 million degrees at its core! And it is brighter than all the lightbulbs on Earth!

# WRITE IT RIGHT

Rewrite each sentence correctly. Use the correct capitalization and punctuation.

**1.** my family went to the beach last saturday

My family went to the beach last Saturday.

**2.** it was a warm and breezy Summer Day

_____

**3.** my Brother carlos swam in the Ocean

_____

**4.** i played in the sand and built a big Sand castle

_____

**5.** carlos and i hunted for shells along the seashore

_____

**6.** we found pink white, and purple shells

_____

**7.** My dad made a big bonfire to cook Dinner

_____

**8.** we ate hot dogs chips and crispy vegetables

_____

**9.** the Ocean smelled fresh and salty

_____

**10.** do you think we can come back next Weekend

_____

_____

## ON YOUR OWN
Write a story about a special day you spent at the beach. If you have never been to the beach, write about a day you'd like to spend there.

 # SHORT WORDS

An **abbreviation** is a shortened word. An abbreviation usually ends with a period. For example, the abbreviation for **August** is **Aug.** Some common abbreviations shorten the names of people, days, and months. Draw a line from each word to its abbreviation.

| | | |
|---|---|---|
| **1.** Missus | Dr. | |
| **2.** Mister | Ms. | |
| **3.** Doctor | Mr. | |
| **4.** Junior | Sr. | |
| **5.** Senior | Mrs. | |
| **6.** Miss/Missus | Jr. | |

**ON YOUR OWN**
On a separate piece of paper, write the days of the week and the months of the year in order.

| | | | | |
|---|---|---|---|---|
| **7.** January | Sat. | **15.** December | Wed. |
| **8.** February | Jan. | **16.** Monday | Mon. |
| **9.** Tuesday | Aug. | **17.** October | Dec. |
| **10.** Thursday | Feb. | **18.** Wednesday | Nov. |
| **11.** August | Sun. | **19.** Friday | Mar. |
| **12.** Sunday | Tues. | **20.** November | Oct. |
| **13.** Saturday | Sept. | **21.** April | Fri. |
| **14.** September | Thurs. | **22.** March | Apr. |

# DRESS FOR THE WEATHER

Circle the names of clothes you would wear in each season.
Some clothes can be worn in more than one season.

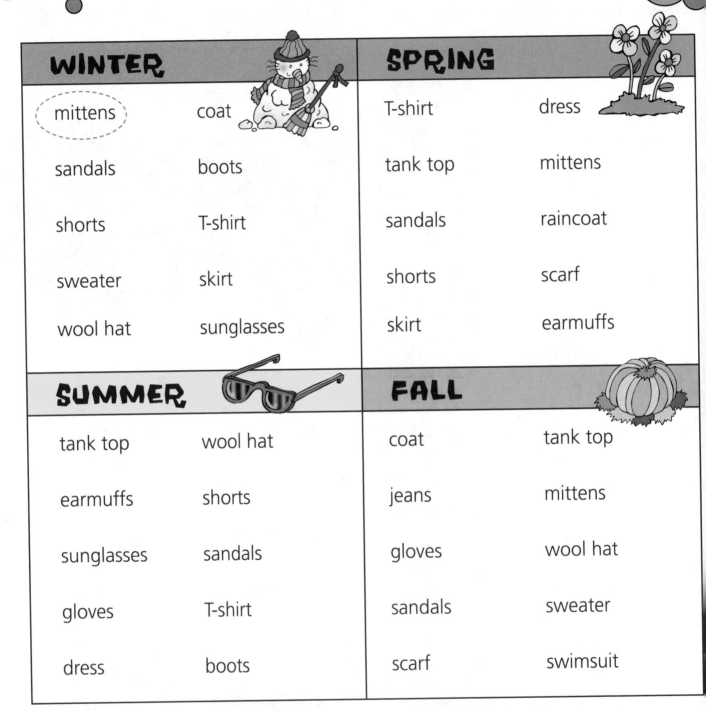

### WINTER

| | |
|---|---|
| (mittens) | coat |
| sandals | boots |
| shorts | T-shirt |
| sweater | skirt |
| wool hat | sunglasses |

### SPRING

| | |
|---|---|
| T-shirt | dress |
| tank top | mittens |
| sandals | raincoat |
| shorts | scarf |
| skirt | earmuffs |

### SUMMER

| | |
|---|---|
| tank top | wool hat |
| earmuffs | shorts |
| sunglasses | sandals |
| gloves | T-shirt |
| dress | boots |

### FALL

| | |
|---|---|
| coat | tank top |
| jeans | mittens |
| gloves | wool hat |
| sandals | sweater |
| scarf | swimsuit |

### ON YOUR OWN

Antarctica is the southern polar ice cap of the Earth. In winter, the Sun does not rise for two weeks. It is like nighttime. In summer, the Sun doesn't set for two weeks. It stays light 24 hours a day!

# WHERE DO I LIVE?

A globe shows oceans and land on Earth. Millions of people live on Earth. They live on different continents and in different countries. Follow the path of the arrows from left to right. It will help you understand where you live in the world. Ask a parent to help you fill in the blanks.

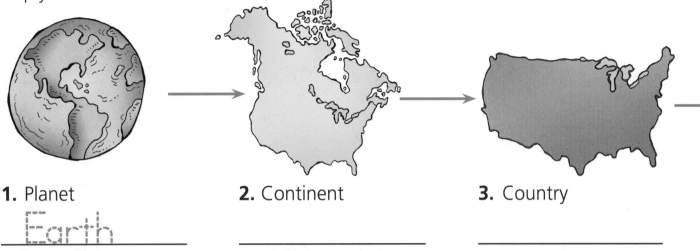

**1.** Planet

Earth
_____

**2.** Continent

_____

**3.** Country

_____

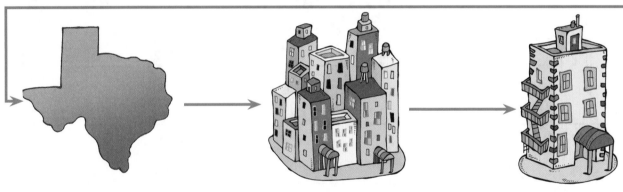

**4.** State

_____

**5.** City or Town

_____

**6.** Street Address

_____

It is a good idea to know where you live. Have a parent help you fill in the information below.

My Full Name: _____

Parents' Names

Mother: _____

Father: _____

Street Address: _____

_____

Phone Number: _____

### ON YOUR OWN
Write emergency numbers for police, fire, ambulance, doctor, and other adults, such as grandparents and friends, on an index card. Keep it with you in case of emergency.

# 100 CHART

Can you count to 100? Fill in the missing numbers in the chart.
When you are done, count aloud from **1** to **100**.

| 1 | ___ | 3 | 4 | 5 | ___ | 7 | ___ | ___ | 10 |
|---|-----|---|---|---|-----|---|-----|-----|----|
| 11 | ___ | 13 | 14 | ___ | 16 | 17 | 18 | ___ | ___ |
| ___ | ___ | 23 | ___ | 25 | 26 | ___ | 28 | ___ | 30 |
| 31 | 32 | 33 | ___ | ___ | 36 | ___ | ___ | 39 | 40 |
| ___ | 42 | 43 | ___ | 45 | 46 | ___ | ___ | 49 | 50 |
| 51 | 52 | ___ | ___ | 55 | ___ | ___ | 58 | ___ | 60 |
| 61 | ___ | ___ | 64 | 65 | 66 | ___ | ___ | ___ | 70 |
| ___ | 72 | 73 | 74 | ___ | ___ | ___ | 78 | 79 | 80 |
| 81 | ___ | 83 | ___ | 85 | 86 | 87 | ___ | 89 | ___ |
| 91 | ___ | ___ | ___ | 95 | 96 | ___ | 98 | 99 | ___ |

**FAST FACT**

There were no crayons, televisions, or computers 100 years ago! Only 8 percent of people owned phones! People washed their hair with egg yolks! The speed limit was 10 miles per hour!

 # DOLLAR DAYS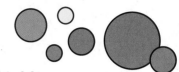

Color the coins in each group that make exactly $1.00.

**1.**

**2.**

**3.**

**4.**

**5.**

## ON YOUR OWN
What can you buy with $1.00? Candy? A coloring book? With a parent, go to a store and list all the things you can buy with $1.00.

# ADVENTURES IN SPACE

Skip count by **5** to finish the picture. What did you draw? Color your picture.

**ON YOUR OWN**
Animals went into space before people did! The first animal to orbit Earth was a Russian dog, named Laika. In 1957, she traveled aboard a spacecraft for 10 days.

# ENDING SENTENCES

Different kinds of sentences have different ending punctuation.

A **statement** ends with a period. (**.**)
A **question** ends with a question mark. (**?**)
An **exclamation** ends with an exclamation mark. (**!**)

For each paragraph, write the correct punctuation mark at the end of each sentence.

**1.** Would you like to come with me to the store I am going to buy new school clothes   I would like to buy new shoes and a coat   After we shop, we can go out to lunch   Do you want burgers or pizza

**2.** Mia and her friends were so excited   They were going to the zoo   At the zoo, they saw all kinds of wild animals   Which do you think was Mia's favorite   Of all the animals, Mia liked the giraffes the best

**3.** Daniel was nervous   Today was the first game of the baseball playoffs   How many games had the Tigers won this season   Daniel was proud they had won all games but one Oh no   It was starting to rain   They would have to wait until tomorrow to play

**ON YOUR OWN**
Write a statement, a question, and an exclamation about summer. Did you use the correct ending punctuation?

# WHAT KIND IS IT?

There are three kinds of sentences.

A **declarative** sentence makes a statement. It ends with a period. (**.**)
**The cat is under the bed.**

An **exclamatory** sentence shows strong feeling or excitement.
It ends with an exclamation mark. (**!**)
**Watch out for that ladder!**

An **interrogative** sentence asks a question. It ends with
a question mark. (**?**)
**Do you want to go to the park?**

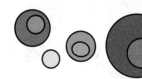

**FAST FACT**
The Sun is not a planet,
like Earth. The Sun is a star!
It is the closest star in the
universe to Earth.

What kinds of sentences are these? Write **D** for **declarative**,
**E** for **exclamatory**, or **I** for **interrogative**.

1. Did you buy milk at the store? _____I_____

2. Justin won first place in the art contest. _____

3. I made my mom a special gift for her birthday. _____

4. Oh no, you stepped in the mud! _____

5. I'm so surprised! _____

6. Dad helped me with my math homework. _____

7. The lion roared loudly from the brush. _____

8. Which kitten would you like to take home? _____

9. Hurry, we'll be late for the bus! _____

10. How many stars can you count in the sky? _____

# ORDER THE STORY

The events in a story are told in a certain order.
Put the sentences for each story in order by writing the numbers **1** to **4**.

**1.**

_3_ When she was clean, Shaggy jumped out of the tub.

_1_ Brandon put Shaggy in the soapy tub.

_2_ He washed Shaggy until he was squeaky-clean.

_4_ Shaggy dried off by shaking water all over Brandon.

**2.**

_____ Elena kicked the winning goal.

_____ The team celebrated and the crowd cheered.

_____ Then she kicked the ball down the field.

_____ Elena got the ball from a teammate.

**3.**

_____ In the spring, Lan planted tomatoes.

_____ She picked the ripe tomatoes and put them in a basket.

_____ Lan gave bags of fresh tomatoes to her neighbors.

_____ The tomato plants grew quickly.

**4.**

_____ Jerome spread peanut butter on the bread.

_____ Jerome felt hungry for a peanut butter sandwich.

_____ He got some bread and peanut butter.

_____ The sandwich was delicious!

## ON YOUR OWN

Look at comic strips in the newspaper.
Each picture is an event in a story. The pictures
must be in a certain order to tell the story. Cut
apart the pictures in a comic strip. Mix them
up. Can you put them in order again?

# CARING FOR OUR WORLD

There are many ways to help care for our world. We can pick up trash, recycle bottles, plant trees, and more! Circle all the children in this picture who are caring for the Earth. Then color the picture.

# ALL ABOUT AMERICA

Complete each sentence about American symbols. Use the words in the word box to help you. Then color the pictures.

| | | |
|---|---|---|
| **"The Star-Spangled Banner"** | **Capitol** | **bald eagle** |
| **Statue of Liberty** | **Liberty Bell** | **flag** |

**1.** This is the _Statue of Liberty_.
It is a symbol of freedom.

**2.** This is a _____
_____.
It is our national bird.

**3.** This is the _____
_____
It is a symbol of liberty.

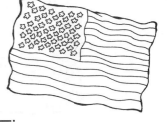

**4.** This the American _____
_____.
It has 50 stars and 13 red and white stripes.

**5.** The name of our national anthem is
_____.
It was written by Francis Scott Key in 1814.

**6.** This is the United States
_____.
It is in Washington, D.C.

**FAST FACT**
Benjamin Franklin didn't want the bald eagle as the national bird. Instead, he wanted the turkey!

# ICE CREAM PARTY

Read the menu at the Polar Bear Ice Cream Shop. Then solve the problems.

## POLAR BEAR ICE CREAM SHOP

| | | | |
|---|---|---|---|
| Single Scoop | 25¢ | Chocolate Sauce | 15¢ |
| Double Scoop | 40¢ | Caramel Sauce | 15¢ |
| Triple Scoop | 55¢ | Candy Sprinkles | 10¢ |
| Banana Split | $1.00 | Cookie Bits | 10¢ |
| Chocolate Sundae | $1.00 | Gummy Bears | 5¢ |

1. Brad got a double scoop with chocolate sauce and cookie bits.
   How much did he spend? 40¢ + 15¢ + 10¢ = 65¢

2. Jacob got a single scoop with caramel sauce.
   How much did he spend? _____

3. Lauren got a chocolate sundae with extra candy sprinkles.
   How much did she spend? _____

4. Jamie got a triple scoop with caramel sauce and gummy bears.
   How much did he spend? _____

5. Mateo got a banana split with extra
   chocolate sauce. How much did he spend?

   _____

**ON YOUR OWN**
What is your favorite snack? Write a sentence describing your favorite snack. Then draw a picture of it.

# DOWN THE SLIDE

Look at the number on each child's shirt. Subtract the numbers down the slide from that number. Write your final answer on the line.

1. ___15-5-3-4-1=2_____

2. _____

3. _____

4. _____

# SHAPE PUZZLE

The numbers below are in a shape puzzle. Use the shape around each number to solve the problems below.

| 2 | 8 | 5 |
|---|---|---|
| 7 | 3 | 1 |
| 4 | 6 | 9 |

**For example:** ⌐ = 9

⌐ + ☐ = 12

1. ⌐9⌐ + ⌐6⌐ + ⌐1⌐ = $\underline{16}$     2. ⌐ + ☐ + ⌐ = _____

3. └ + └ + ⌐ = _____     4. ☐ + ⌐ + ⌐ = _____

5. └┘ + └ + ☐ = _____     6. └ + └ + ⌐ = _____

7. ⌐ + └ + ⌐ = _____     8. ⌐ + └┘ + ☐ = _____

9. ⌐ + ⌐ + ⌐ = _____     10. ☐ + ☐ + └ = _____

11. └┘ + ⌐ + ☐ = _____

12. ⌐ + ⌐ + ⌐ = _____

48

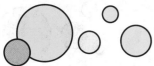 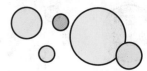

Look at the bold words in each sentence. Find the letter that is in the first two words, but not in the last word. Write that letter in the box. When you are done, read the letters from top to bottom. What is the secret word?

1. It is in **dig** and **hand**, but not in **cat**.  `d`

2. It is in **wild** and **pig**, but not in **laugh**.  ⬜

3. It is in **name** and **knit**, but not in **baby**.  ⬜

4. It is in **coat** and **oven**, but not in **car**.  ⬜

5. It is in **wish** and **snake**, but not in **meat**.  ⬜

6. It is in **wait** and **lamb**, but not in **dog**.  ⬜

7. It is in **bump** and **huge**, but not in **love**.  ⬜

8. It is in **rain** and **tire**, but not in **ice**.  ⬜

What is the secret word?  _____

Draw a picture of the secret word below.

**FAST FACT**
Diplodocus was over 90 feet long! That's almost as long as three school buses!

49

# IN THE DICTIONARY

In the dictionary, words are in alphabetical order. If words have the same first letter, look at the second letter. Write each group of words in alphabetical order.

**1.**

apple    always
ace       after

ace
after
always
apple

**2.**

book    brook
blank   ball

_____
_____
_____
_____

**3.**

creek   clown
cold    cave

_____
_____
_____
_____

**4.**

day       drain
dinner   desk

_____
_____
_____
_____

**5.**

proud    plane
people   pail

_____
_____
_____
_____

**6.**

rhino    racoon
rust     roam

_____
_____
_____
_____

## FAST FACT

You can find a lot more than the meaning of a word in a dictionary. You can find the part of speech, pronunciation, origin, spelling, example sentences, and much more.

**7.**

story    slide
snake    sale

_____
_____
_____
_____

**8.**

trail    team
tool     tide

_____
_____
_____
_____

# IN THE MEADOW

Read the paragraph. Then answer the questions.

I will never forget last summer. My family went on a camping trip to the mountains. We set up our tent next to a big, beautiful meadow. The meadow was filled with yellow flowers. Each night, I fell asleep to the sounds of croaking frogs and chirping crickets. One morning, I went on a walk in the meadow. I watched bees buzzing around the flowers. I felt the warm sun on my back. Then right in front of me, I saw a doe and her fawn. I stood without moving. I hoped they would stay, but they did not. They ran off into the woods. It lasted only a few moments. I will never forget the deer in the meadow.

1. When did my family go camping? _____

2. Where did my family go camping? _____

3. What filled the meadow? _____

4. What special thing did I see in the meadow? _____

5. What sounds did I hear as I was falling asleep?

_____

_____

_____

**ON YOUR OWN**
Have you ever gone camping? Write a description of what you saw, heard, smelled, and felt.

51

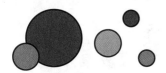

# ANIMAL GROUPS

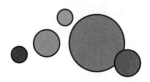

Animals belong to special groups.

Most **mammals** live on land. Mammals are warm-blooded and have fur. They give birth to live young.

Some **reptiles** live on land and some live in water. They are cold-blooded and have scales. They lay eggs.

**Fish** live in water. Fish have scales and breathe through gills. They lay eggs.

**Birds** live on land. Birds have feathers and wings, but not all can fly. They lay eggs.

Write these animal names in the correct column below.

| | | | |
|---|---|---|---|
| **chicken** | **rattlesnake** | **lizard** | **robin** |
| **alligator** | **eagle** | **monkey** | **dinosaur** |
| **catfish** | **deer** | **tuna** | **eel** |
| **skunk** | **parrot** | **trout** | **lion** |

| MAMMALS | REPTILES | FISH | BIRDS |
|---|---|---|---|
| skunk | | | |
| | | | |
| | | | |
| | | | |

# MANNERS MATTER

Good manners help people get along with each other. Complete each sentence with a word from the box. Use your answers to complete the crossword puzzle.

**love**

**thank you**

**sorry**

**shake**

**may**

**open**

**smile**

**please**

**nice**

**excuse**

Across 1: t h a n k y o u

## ACROSS

**1.** When you receive a gift, you say, "_____."

**4.** It is polite to _____ the door for people.

**7.** When you ask a favor, you always say, "_____."

**9.** When you are asking permission to do something, say, "_____ I?"

## DOWN

**2.** When you meet someone, you say, "_____ to meet you."

**3.** When you do something wrong, you say, "I'm _____."

**5.** When you need to get by someone, you say, "_____me."

**6.** People like to see a friendly _____ on your face.

**8.** Say "I _____ you" to the people you care about.

**10.** When you meet people, it is polite to _____ their hand.

### ON YOUR OWN

Think about a time when you had to say, "I'm sorry." What happened? Did you feel better after apologizing? Draw a picture to show what happened.

There are different ways to write time.

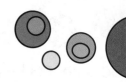

**2:15**
**quarter past two**
**15 minutes after 2**

Draw lines to match the times in all three columns.

2:30

quarter past 5

one-thirty

11:15

12 o'clock

7 o'clock

noon

1:30

5:15

half past 2

7:00

15 minutes after 11

# ESTIMATION STATION

An **estimation** is a guess based on what you know. Estimate the price for each item. Circle your answer.

**1.**

($40)　　**$400**

**2.**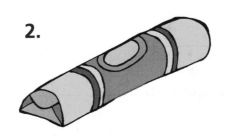

**$7.50**　　**75¢**

**3.**

**$1.50**　　**$10.50**

**4.**

**$12**　　**$120**

**5.**

**$15,000**　　**$50**

**6.**

**$150**　　**$15**

**7.**

**$500**　　**$5**

**8.**

**$10**　　**$1**

## ON YOUR OWN

Try to estimate the cost of things you see every day, like a pencil, apple, or toothbrush. What about cookies, socks, or stamps? Ask a parent to help you find out if your estimates are correct.

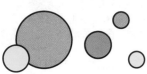

# FAVORITE COOKIES

Look at the graph. Then answer the questions.

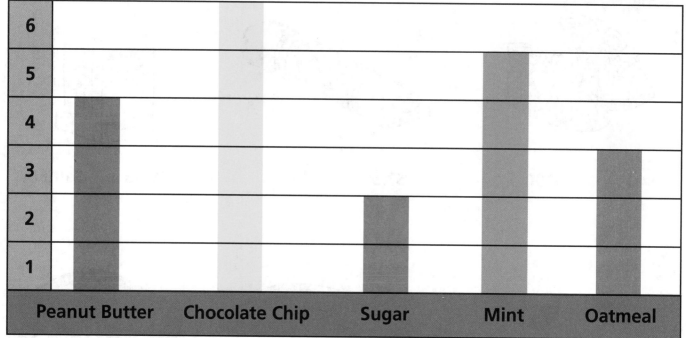

**Kinds of Cookies**

1. Which cookie do children like best? _chocolate chip_

2. Which cookie do children like least? _____

3. How many children like mint cookies? _____

4. How many more children like chocolate chip cookies than sugar cookies? _____

5. Do more children like peanut butter cookies or oatmeal cookies? _____

**ON YOUR OWN**
With a parent, make your favorite cookie recipe. Help measure ingredients using measuring cups and spoons.

# UNDER THE SEA

Color the verbs **green**.
Color the nouns **blue**.
Color the adjectives **orange**.
Color all the other words **red**.

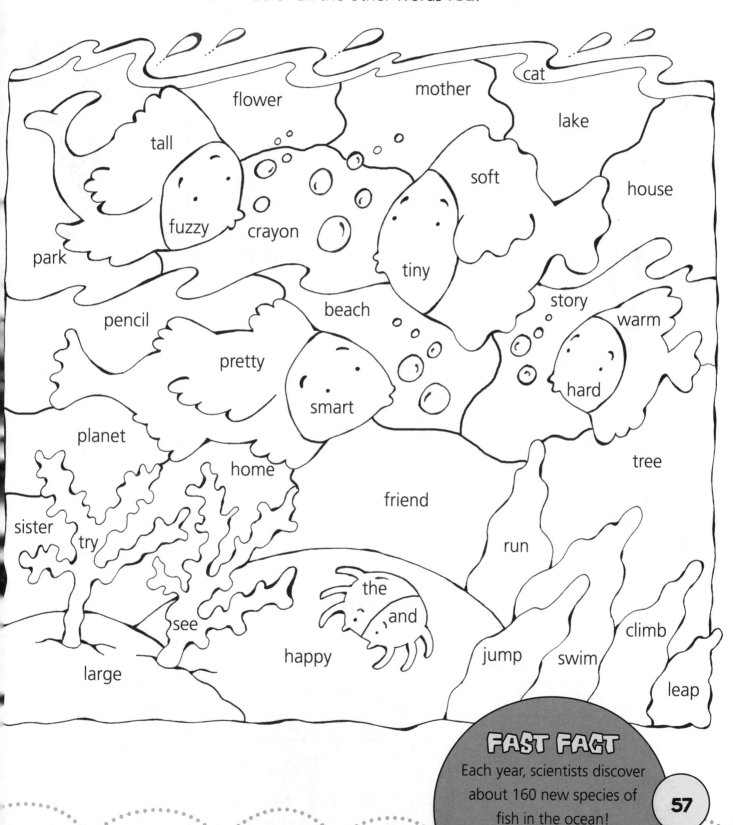

flower
mother
cat
lake
tall
soft
house
fuzzy
crayon
tiny
park
story
pencil
beach
warm
pretty
hard
smart
planet
home
tree
friend
sister
try
run
see
the
and
climb
happy
jump
swim
large
leap

# SOLVE THE RIDDLE

Look at the bold words in each sentence. Find the letter that is in the first two words, but not in the last word. Write that letter in the box. When you are done, read the letters from top to bottom. If you are correct, you will solve the riddle.

**The more of them you take, the more you leave behind.**
Write the letters on the lines below.

1. It is in **frog** and **fan**, but not in **sit**. `f`

2. It is in **hop** and **cot**, but not in **ace**.

3. It is in **mop** and **boat**, but not in **kite**.

4. It is in **tan** and **top**, but not in **mud**.

5. It is in **sit** and **ask**, but not in **me**.

6. It is in **bat** and **ten**, but not in **dog**.

7. It is in **eel** and **eat**, but not in **soap**.

8. It is in **pin** and **map**, but not in **bed**.

9. It is in **sea** and **sun**, but not in **wet**.

**Answer:**

\_\_\_ \_\_\_ \_\_\_ \_\_\_ \_\_\_ \_\_\_ \_\_\_ \_\_\_ \_\_\_

**ON YOUR OWN**
Come up with your own riddle for someone to solve.

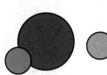
# BUSY BALLOONS

Many words have opposite meanings. For example, **hot** and **cold** are opposites. Find words with opposite meanings on the balloons. Color the balloon pairs the same color.

happy

quiet

big

begin

empty

loud

full

end

sweet

sad

small

sour

**ON YOUR OWN**
What other opposites can you think of? Make a list of opposites. Then draw simple pictures or symbols to show what they mean.

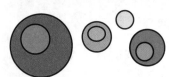 # GOING PLACES

Write the name of each vehicle under the picture. Use the words in the box to help you. Draw vehicles in the scene on page 61. Put them on land, in water, or in the air. Then color the picture.

| | | | |
|---|---|---|---|
| helicopter | sailboat | car | truck |
| airplane | train | bicycle | ship |
| hot air balloon | motorcycle | scooter | skateboard |

**1.**

_car_

**2.**

_____

**3.**

_____

**4.**

_____

**5.**

_____

**6.**

_____

**7.**

_____

**8.**

_____

**9.**

_____

**10.**

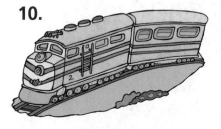

_____

**11.**

_____

**12.**

_____

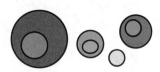 

# MIXING COLORS

If you mix certain colors, you can make new colors! See how many new colors you can make by solving each color problem. Color the paint can the new color.

**1.**

blue + yellow = _green_

**2.**

red + white = _____

**3.**

red + blue = _____

**4.**

red + yellow = _____

**5.**

black + white = _____

**ON YOUR OWN**

Experiment with color. Use a set of finger paints to mix together different colors. Make up names for all the new colors you make.

**6.** Now, mix your own two colors! Write the colors below. Then color the can your new color.

_____ + _____ = _____

# TENS AND ONES

**In the number 12:**
1 stands for one group of ten
2 stands for the number of extras

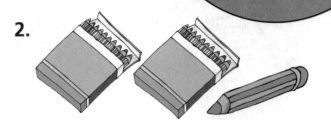

**ON YOUR OWN**
Get a bag of candy, beans, or buttons. Count them by grouping them into tens. Then count the extras. How many did you count in total?

Look at the pictures below. Write how many groups of ten and how many extras there are in each number.

**1.**

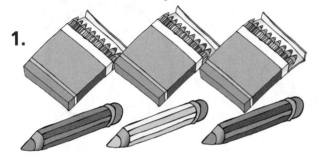

33 = __3__ __3__
      tens    ones

**2.**

21 = _____ _____
      tens    ones

**3.**

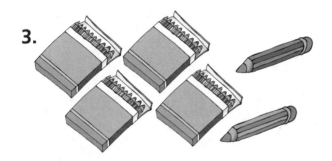

42 = _____ _____
      tens    ones

**4.**

15 = _____ _____
      tens    ones

**5.**

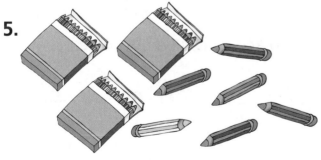

36 = _____ _____
      tens    ones

**6.**

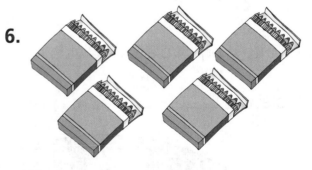

50 = _____ _____
      tens    ones

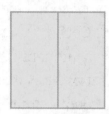

Fractions help you divide things into equal parts. Draw lines to divide each food into equal parts. Write the fraction. Then color each piece a different color.

**1 whole = 2 halves ($\frac{1}{2}$)**
**(2 equal pieces)**

**1 whole = 4 fourths ($\frac{1}{4}$)**
**(4 equal pieces)**

**1.**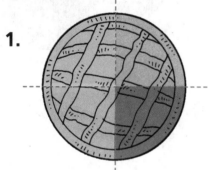

**2.**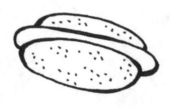

**3.**

Divide into 4 equal pieces.

Divide into 2 equal pieces.

Divide into 2 equal pieces.

Each piece = _____

Each piece = _____

Each piece = _____

**4.**

**5.**

**6.**

Divide into 4 equal pieces.

Divide into 2 equal pieces.

Divide into 4 equal pieces.

Each piece = _____

Each piece = _____

Each piece = _____

## ON YOUR OWN

Get some real food to divide into equal pieces. Divide a piece of bread into fourths. Divide a big cookie into halves. Have a parent help you divide an apple or orange into halves or fourths.

# TOOLS OF THE TRADE

We use different tools to measure weight, length, temperature, and volume. Look at these measuring tools below. Then write which tool you would use to measure each item.

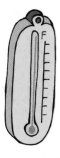
**thermometer**

**measuring cup**

**scale**

**ruler**

**1.** Amount of flour to add to cookie batter

Tool: __measuring cup__

**2.** Temperature of ice water

Tool: _____

**3.** Length of a room

Tool: _____

**4.** Your height

Tool: _____

**5.** Weight of tomatoes at the market

Tool: _____

**6.** Amount of oatmeal to add to boiling water

Tool: _____

**7.** Temperature of the air outdoors

Tool: _____

**8.** Weight of a chicken

Tool: _____

## ON YOUR OWN

Get some measuring cups and spoons. Ask a parent to help you practice measuring different amounts of rice and water. Then prepare a recipe together!

# FOLLOWING DIRECTIONS

Directions must be written in a certain order to make sense. Write numbers **1** to **5** to put each set of directions in the correct order.

**1.**

_____ Put a pot of water on the stove to boil.

_____ Pour the tomato sauce over cooked pasta.

_____ Put the pasta in the boiling water.

_____ As pasta is cooking, heat up tomato sauce.

_____ Drain pasta, and put it in a bowl.

What did you make? _____

**ON YOUR OWN**
Write directions for something you know how to do. Number each step. Ask a friend to read your directions. Do they make sense?

**2.**

_____ Put your toothbrush away.

_____ Rinse off your toothbrush.

_____ Brush your teeth.

_____ Take out your toothbrush and toothpaste.

_____ Put toothpaste on your toothbrush.

What did you do? _____

**3.**

_____ Open the jam jar.

_____ Put bread in the toaster.

_____ Spread jam on the toasted bread.

_____ Take out bread, jam, and a knife.

_____ Take bread out of the toaster.

What did you make? _____

# CONTRACTION ACTION

A **contraction** is a short word made up of two other words. The missing letter or letters are replaced with an apostrophe (').

**I + am = I'm**         **did + not = didn't**         **will not = won't**

Draw a line to match each contraction to the two words it is made from.

| | |
|---|---|
| can't | I am |
| we'll | can not |
| they're | she is |
| don't | he is |
| I'm | they are |
| he's | we will |
| I'll | I will |
| she's | do not |

## ON YOUR OWN
Write contractions on one set of index cards. Write the two words that make up the contractions on another set of index cards. Practice matching the two sets of cards.

# THE AMAZING KANGAROO

Read about kangaroos. Then answer the questions.

When people think of Australia, they often think of kangaroos. Kangaroos are amazing animals. They use their powerful hind legs to jump great lengths. They can jump the length of a school bus! Kangaroos belong to a special group of animals called marsupials. Marsupials carry their babies in pouches. Baby kangaroos have a special name, too. They are called joeys. When a joey is born, it is only the size of a single pea. This tiny newborn stays in its mother's pouch for ten months. Then it comes out to explore the world. Even when a joey is too big for its mother's pouch, it will jump back in if it is scared!

1. Where do kangaroos live? _____ Australia _____

2. To what group of animals do kangaroos belong? _____

3. Finish this sentence:
   Marsupials carry their babies in _____.

4. What is a baby kangaroo called? _____

5. How long does a baby kangaroo stay in its mother's pouch?

   _____

**FAST FACT**
Male kangaroos are called boomers. Female kangaroos are called flyers. A group of kangaroos is called a mob.

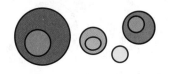

# LIFE CYCLE OF A BUTTERFLY

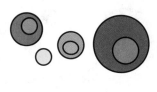

The life cycle of a butterfly has four stages. Write **1** to **4** to put the stages in order.

_____ **Caterpillar:** This plump creature eats and eats. It splits and sheds its skin many times.

_____ **Butterfly:** This pretty insect comes out of the pupa, totally changed.

_____ **Pupa:** The caterpillar attaches itself to a plant and forms a hard shell.

___1___ **Egg:** This is laid by a female butterfly and left on a plant to hatch.

**FAST FACT**
A caterpillar can take up to five hours to shed its skin. That's a lot of wriggling and twisting!

Fill in the life cycle below. Draw and label a picture of each stage.

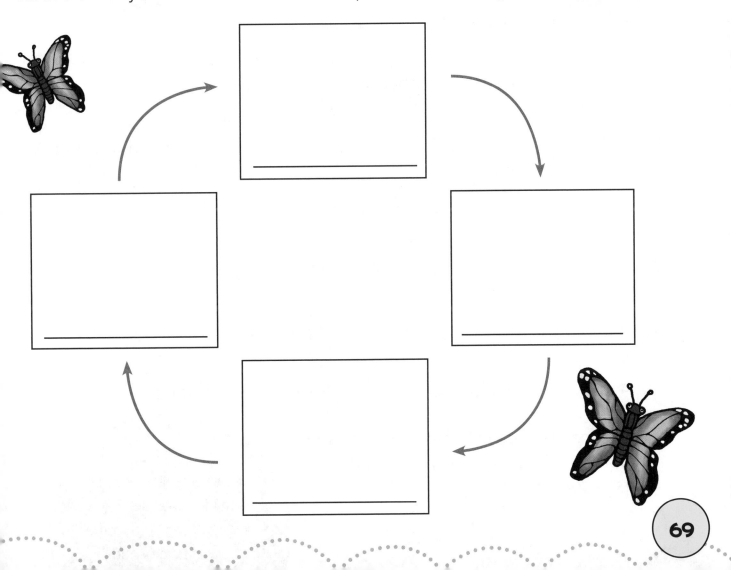

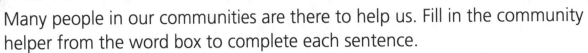

# IN MY COMMUNITY

Many people in our communities are there to help us. Fill in the community helper from the word box to complete each sentence.

| police officer | firefighter | nurse | veterinarian | teacher |
| mail carrier | clerk | doctor | bus driver | dentist |

1. A __firefighter__ rescues people and puts out fires.

2. At school, my _____ shows me how to read and write.

3. The _____ delivers mail to my home.

4. When my pet is sick, I take it to a _____ .

5. When I am sick or need a checkup, I go see my _____ .

6. At the market, the _____ helps me find and buy food.

7. The _____ takes me to school on the bus.

8. My _____ helps me to keep my teeth healthy.

9. A _____ helps a doctor in many ways.

10. A _____ fights crime and helps me stay safe.

On a separate piece of paper, draw a picture of your favorite community helper. Show this person doing his or her job.

**FAST FACT**

Some veterinarians work only with big animals. They spend their time driving out to farms to treat cows, horses, and pigs!

# COLOR BY NUMBER

Solve each subtraction problem. Then use the Color Key to color the picture.

## FAST FACT

The Tyrannosaurus rex's teeth were 9 to 13 inches long! They were razor sharp, which helped the T-Rex eat about 500 pounds of meat with each bite!

## COLOR KEY

Answers 0 – 2 = **green**

Answers 3 – 5 = **brown**

Answers 6 – 8 = **yellow**

Answers 9 – 11 = **blue**

# MORNING, AFTERNOON, AND NIGHT

People usually do things during certain times of the day or night. Circle **morning**, **afternoon**, or **night** to tell when you do each activity below.

| | | | | |
|---|---|---|---|---|
| **1.** | I eat dinner. | morning | afternoon | (night) |
| **2.** | I get home from school. | morning | afternoon | night |
| **3.** | I leave for school. | morning | afternoon | night |
| **4.** | I eat breakfast. | morning | afternoon | night |
| **5.** | I go to sleep. | morning | afternoon | night |
| **6.** | I eat lunch. | morning | afternoon | night |
| **7.** | I take a bath. | morning | afternoon | night |
| **8.** | I put on my pajamas. | morning | afternoon | night |

### ON YOUR OWN
Fold a piece of paper in half. Label one side **Morning** and the other side **Night**. Then draw yourself doing something in the morning and at night.

# SHOP 'TIL YOU DROP!

Read each story problem below. Then circle **yes** or **no** to answer the question.

**1.** The baseball costs 75¢.
You have:

Do you have enough money?
**(yes)** **no**

**2.** The candy costs 60¢
You have:

Do you have enough money?
**yes** **no**

**3.** The movie costs 40¢.
You have:

Do you have enough money?
**yes** **no**

**4.** The flowers cost 99¢.
You have:

Do you have enough money?
**yes** **no**

**5.** The hamburger costs 57¢.
You have:

Do you have enough money?
**yes** **no**

**6.** The doll costs 85¢.
You have:

Do you have enough money?
**yes** **no**

## FAST FACT
Would you trade your baseball cards for a loaf of bread? Before people used money, they traded things to get what they needed.

# PICTURE THIS!

Pictures can help us when we read. Look carefully at this picture. Then circle the correct answer for each question.

**1.** What is the girl in the hat doing?

    a) surfing      (b) reading)      c) singing      d) sleeping

**2.** Where does this scene take place?

    a) park      b) mountains      c) house      d) beach

**3.** What are the mother and boy eating for lunch?

    a) sandwiches      b) chicken      c) hot dogs      d) pizza

**4.** What is the girl collecting in her bucket?

    a) shells      b) rocks

    c) books      d) sand

**5.** Someone is in the water. What is he doing?

    a) swimming      b) surfing

    c) sleeping      d) floating

### ON YOUR OWN

Write a story about the picture. What kind of day is it? Who are the people in the picture? Are they having fun? Where are they going after they leave?

 # ZOO MIX-UP

These zoo animals' names are all mixed up! Unscramble the letters to spell each animal's name correctly.

1. e r b a _____ bear _____

2. a a k o l _____

3. i r a g f e f _____

4. h i r n o _____

5. t g i r e _____

6. b z r a e _____

7. n s a e k _____

8. e h l e a p t n _____

9. a p n a d _____

10. o n l i _____

11. y m n k o e _____

12. p i h p o _____

## BONUS WORD

Can you figure out this animal?

l i g a l a r t o

_____

## ON YOUR OWN

What is your favorite zoo animal? Draw a picture of it. Ask your parent to help you find facts about this animal. Then write a few sentences about the animal, telling where it lives, what it eats, and more.

Good writing has good descriptions. **Adjectives** are describing words. Write three adjectives to describe each picture below. Try to use the best words you can.

soft
playful
cute

## ON YOUR OWN

Look at one of your favorite toys. Write as many descriptive words as you can about it. Think of color, shape, size, and texture.

# PRECIOUS PETS

Owning a pet is a big responsibility. Pets need many things to live long and happy lives. Unscramble the word in each sentence to tell how you should care for a pet. Write the word on the line.

**1.** Give your pet a **T B H A** to keep it clean.    *bath*

**2.** Make sure your pet gets its shots from the **T V E** .    _____

**3.** Give your pet fresh **T R W A E** every day.    _____

**4.** Some pets enjoy **A L W K S** for exercise.    _____

**5.** Pets need good **O F O D** to stay strong and healthy.    _____

**6.** Make time to have fun and **A P L Y** with your pet.    _____

**7.** Most of all, give your pet lots of care and **V E O L** .    _____

Find and circle the words above in the word search.
Words can go across or down.

| P | L | A | Y | U | W | A |
|---|---|---|---|---|---|---|
| F | O | N | W | F | A | R |
| A | V | L | P | O | L | W |
| V | E | T | B | O | K | U |
| R | E | M | A | D | S | E |
| E | W | A | T | E | R | T |
| S | O | T | H | A | C | H |

**FAST FACT**
Some people own unusual pets, such as skunks, ferrets, pot-bellied pigs, chameleons, and even crickets!

# LET'S CELEBRATE!

All families celebrate special events and holidays. In the quilt below, draw four pictures of special times or celebrations you shared with your family. Think of holidays, birthdays, parties, and more! Label each picture. Then color the quilt.

## ON YOUR OWN
Think of someone in your family who does nice things for you. Make him or her a thank-you card!

# RIDDLE FUN

Write the answer to the problem in each box. Then use the Answer Key to find the letter that matches the answer. Write the letter on the line below to answer the riddle.

**Answer Key**

| 1 | 2 | 3 | 4 | 5 | 6 | 7 | 8 | 9 | 10 |
|---|---|---|---|---|---|---|---|---|----|
| D | K | R | U | T | O | E | Y | N | M |

**Name three keys that don't unlock doors.**

| 15 – 5 | 14 – 8 | 13 – 4 | 8 – 6 | 12 – 5 | 10 – 2 |
|--------|--------|--------|-------|--------|--------|
| 10 |  |  |  |  |  |

M ___ ___ ___ ___ ___

| 8 – 3 | 10 – 6 | 11 – 8 | 9 – 7 | 8 – 1 | 14 – 6 |
|-------|--------|--------|-------|-------|--------|
|  |  |  |  |  |  |

___ ___ ___ ___ ___ ___

| 6 – 5 | 11 – 5 | 16 – 7 | 5 – 3 | 14 – 7 | 13 – 5 |
|-------|--------|--------|-------|--------|--------|
|  |  |  |  |  |  |

___ ___ ___ ___ ___ ___

**FAST FACT**

Monkeys are very much like humans. Like us, they have thumbs, which allow them to hold and use many different tools.

# MOUNTAIN CHALLENGE

Help Benny Bear climb the mountain. First, solve the addition problems. Color the sums that are even numbers to find a path for Benny. Then color the picture.

### FAST FACT

How do bears survive when they hibernate? They spend several months eating in order to gain weight. They can gain up to 40 pounds of fat per week! The bear uses all this stored energy as food when it's hibernating.

8 + 4 =

7 + 7 =

3 + 2 =

5 + 5 =

3 + 4 =

8 + 8 =

5 + 1 =

5 + 4 =

8 + 9 =

2 + 2 =

8 + 4 =

6 + 7 =

8 + 3 =

3 + 7 =

5 + 6 =

9 + 9 =

4 + 4 =

8 + 7 =

9 + 4 =

# BEFORE AND AFTER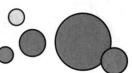

Fill in the missing numbers by counting forward.

**1.** 33 __34__ 35

**2.** 29 _____ 31

**3.** 54 55 _____

**4.** 16 _____ _____ 19

**5.** 48 _____ 50 _____

**6.** 32 33 _____ _____

**7.** 96 _____ 98 _____ _____

**8.** 61 62 _____ _____ _____

Fill in the missing numbers by counting backward.

**9.** 67 __66__ 65

**10.** 91 90 _____

**11.** 20 _____ 18

**12.** 72 71 _____ _____

**13.** 80 _____ _____ 77

**14.** 57 _____ 55 _____

**15.** 29 _____ _____ 26 _____

**16.** 44 _____ 42 _____ _____

## ON YOUR OWN

Use this idea of "before and after" to test yourself in other areas. For example, what is a dog before it grows up? A puppy! What meal do you eat after lunch? Dinner!

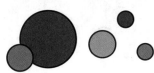

# VIBRANT VOWELS

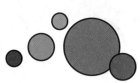

Short vowels sound like:

a in **cat**    e in **ten**    i in **pin**    o in **top**    u in **bug**

Long vowels sound like:

a in **lake**    e in **eat**    i in **like**    o in **boat**    u in **blue**

Read each word in the box. If the word has the short vowel sound, write it in a spot on the top of the egg. If the word has the long vowel sound, write it in a spot on the bottom of the egg.

**tune**

**cone**

**cub**

**mail**

**neat**

**fog**

**grab**

**lime**

**shell**

**hid**

Guess what is in the egg! Unscramble the letters to find out. Here's a hint: The word has the **long a** sound.

E    A    N    K    S

Answer: _____

**ON YOUR OWN**

What other animals hatch from eggs? Do some research to find out. Remember, reptiles, birds, and fish all lay eggs.

# IN THE GROUP

Read each group of words. Then circle the word that does not belong.
Color the shell **blue** if the words are nouns.
Color the shell **green** if the words are adjectives.
Color the shell **yellow** if the words are verbs.

1. red
   pink
   round
   blue

2. girl
   animal
   boy
   baby

3. sad
   happy
   tall
   angry

4. water
   apple
   orange
   peach

5. run
   sleep
   walk
   skip

6. cat
   dog
   mouse
   father

7. huge
   big
   tiny
   large

8. steak
   soda
   juice
   milk

9. tulip
   daisy
   bee
   rose

10. sweet
    tired
    spicy
    sour

11. hop
    jump
    leap
    sit

12. sister
    desk
    teacher
    student

**FAST FACT**

Animals with shells are called **crustaceans**. Snails, crabs, lobsters, and shrimp are all crustaceans.

83

# HEARING SYLLABLES

Every word is made up of syllables. Say these words aloud slowly. Clap on each syllable. Look at how the lines separate each word into syllables.

**car** ☐1        **rabbit** (rab / bit) ☐2        **December** (De / cem / ber) ☐3

Read each word aloud slowly. Clap on the syllables. Then write the number of syllables in the box. Draw lines to show the syllables.

1. doc / tor ☐2          2. buck ☐          3. rooster ☐

4. wheat ☐             5. November ☐      6. Saturday ☐

7. person ☐            8. instead ☐       9. myself ☐

10. understand ☐      11. public ☐        12. bulldozer ☐

Find the words with two syllables in the word search. Words can go across or down. You should find six words.

| P | A | T | R | O | S | U | P |
|---|---|---|---|---|---|---|---|
| U | W | E | O | A | P | C | E |
| B | R | D | O | C | T | O | R |
| L | E | A | S | B | A | I | S |
| I | N | S | T | E | A | D | O |
| C | U | M | E | I | V | J | N |
| R | P | E | R | D | I | Y | O |
| T | A | M | Y | S | E | L | F |

**ON YOUR OWN**
Write down the names of your family members and friends. Draw lines to separate the names into syllables.

84

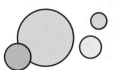

# LET'S GET HEALTHY!

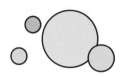

These are all healthy foods:

**breads and grains**          **meats**

**vegetables and fruits**      **dairy foods** (milk and cheese)

Some foods are not good for you.
These foods are okay to eat sometimes:

**fats** (greasy foods)          **sweets** (candy)

**ON YOUR OWN**
Write down all the food you eat for one whole day. Are you eating the right amount of healthy foods? What foods should you add to your diet?

Look at the foods below. Circle the food if it is a healthy food.
Draw an **X** over the food if it is not healthy.

# BIRTHDAY

With a parent's help, fill out this birth certificate. Tape a baby picture in the box, or draw a picture of yourself as a baby.

First Name: _____

Middle Name: _____

Last Name: _____

Who named me?_____

What does my name mean? _____

Date of Birth: _____

Day of the Week: _____

Time: _____

Weight: _____ Length: _____

My hair color was: _____

My eye color was: _____

When I was born, I looked the most like: _____

Hospital and hometown: _____

Mother's Name: _____

Father's Name: _____

## ON YOUR OWN
Find out more about the day and year you were born. What gifts did you receive? Who was the first person to hold you? What songs were popular? Who was president of the United States? Make a scrapbook of your findings!

# FAVORITE VACATION

Many people take vacations in the summer. Complete the graph below by asking six people about their favorite vacation spot. Color a square for each answer. Start at the bottom of the graph. Then answer the questions below.

| Number of People | Beach | Mountains | Country | City |
|---|---|---|---|---|
| 6 | | | | |
| 5 | | | | |
| 4 | | | | |
| 3 | | | | |
| 2 | | | | |
| 1 | | | | |

**Vacation Places**

1. Which place did people like best? _____

2. Which place did people like least? _____

3. Which place did people like second best? _____

4. What did you learn from making this graph? _____

_____

**ON YOUR OWN**
Make another graph to find different information. You can find out people's favorite ice cream, season, TV show, animal, and more!

# PACKING PEANUTS

There are 10 peanuts in each bag. Circle each group of 10 peanuts. Count the extras, then write the numbers on the lines.

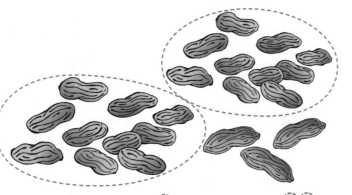

1. __2__ __3__ = __23__
   tens    ones

2. _____ _____ = _____
     tens     ones

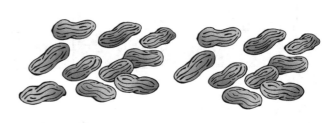

3. _____ _____ = _____
     tens     ones

4. _____ _____ = _____
     tens     ones

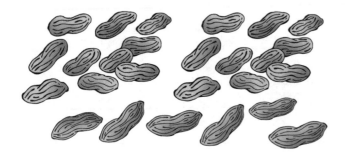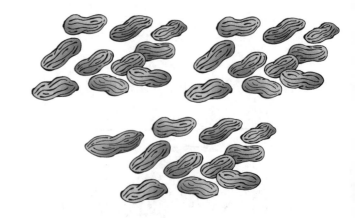

5. _____ _____ = _____
     tens     ones

6. _____ _____ = _____
     tens     ones

## ON YOUR OWN

Write addition problems using the tens and ones on this page. Use problem 1 as an example: **20 + 3 = 23**.

# PATH TO POETRY

Finish each poem below by writing a word from the box. Choose a word that rhymes with the last word in the first sentence.

| song | trees | care | feet |
|------|-------|------|------|

**1.** My little cat is soft and sweet,

She plays with yarn with her tiny ___feet___.

**2.** I love the summer days so long,

I hear birds sing a happy _____.

**3.** Pumpkins, scarecrows, chilly breeze,

Colored leaves fall from the _____.

**4.** Sandy beach and salty air,

In the warm sun without a _____.

### ON YOUR OWN
Read some Mother Goose rhymes and poems. Try to write a poem copying the style of one of the poems you read.

Now write your own poem! Think of summer days, friends, and things you like to do. Below are some rhyming word pairs to help you.

| fun / sun | pool / cool | snug / bug | light / kite | sky / fly | day / play |
|-----------|-------------|------------|--------------|-----------|------------|

_____ ,

_____ .

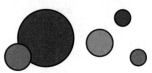
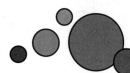

# DEAR FRIEND

Write a letter to a friend! Tell your friend about the things you are doing this summer. Then color it and give it to your friend to read.

_____ (date)

Dear _____ ,

Your friend,

_____

# SINK OR FLOAT?

Some things will float on water, and some won't. What objects do you think will sink? What objects do you think will float? Find out by doing this experiment!

1. Gather the items shown below.
2. Fill a tub or bucket with water.
3. One at time, place the objects in the water.
4. Color the object below if it floats.
5. Cross out the object below if it sinks.

**feather**

leaf

**penny**

**rock**

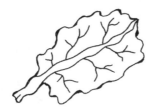

**twig**

**crayon**

**paper clip**

**flower**

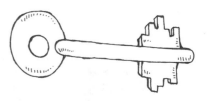

**key**

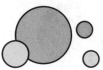

# SUMMER READING LIST

Here are some books for readers going into second grade to enjoy during the summer months.

***Why Mosquitoes Buzz in People's Ears:***
***A West African Tale*** by Verna Aardema
Illustrated by Leo and Diane Dillon
This African folktale begins when a mosquito teases an iguana, causing the iguana to panic. The panic spreads in this delightful tale, illustrated with an African motif.

***The Babe & I*** by David A. Adler
Illustrated by Terry Widener
While selling newspapers to help his family during the Great Depression, a young boy meets his idol, Babe Ruth.

***Freckle Juice*** by Judy Blume, Illustrated by Sonia O. Lisker
Andrew wants freckles more than anything in the world, so Sharon sells him her secret freckle juice recipe. Unfortunately, Andrew runs into a few problems while trying to give himself freckles!

***Abuela (Grandmother)*** by Arthur Dorros
Illustrated by Elisa Kleven
During a visit with her grandmother, a young girl imagines she is flying above New York City, seeing all the famous landmarks. Spanish words are integrated into the dialogue.

***The Doorbell Rang*** Written and Illustrated by Pat Hutchins
Sam and Victoria must share a dozen cookies with their friends. This book reinforces math skills, as the cookies must be divided again and again!

***Wilma Unlimited: How Wilma Rudolph Became the World's Fastest Woman*** by Kathleen Krull
Illustrated by David Diaz
Wilma Rudolph is only five years old when she contracts polio. Never expected to walk again, Wilma becomes the first American woman to win three gold medals in the 1960 Olympic games.

***Brown Bear, Brown Bear, What Do You See?***
by Bill Martin, Jr., Illustrated by Eric Carle
Beautiful tissue-paper collages and rhythmic text make this a children's classic. Each page introduces a new animal, using rhymes that make it easy for children to read along.

***The Paper Bag Princess*** by Robert Munsch
Illustrated by Michael Martchenko
Princess Elizabeth must wear a paper bag after her clothes are burned by a dragon. Undaunted, she rescues the prince, who scorns her "paper bag" gown. Elizabeth's response will delight feisty females everywhere!

***If You Give a Mouse a Cookie*** by Laura J. Numeroff
Illustrated by Felicia Bond
If you give a mouse a cookie, he'll want a glass of milk. Then he'll want a straw, and more! Multiple favors build upon each other until a young child is exhausted!

***The True Story of the 3 Little Pigs*** by Jon Scieszka
Illustrated by Lane Smith
Told from the viewpoint of the "poor" Wolf, children will delight in this retelling of the classic tale.

***Sagwa, The Chinese Siamese Cat*** by Amy Tan
Illustrated by Gretchen Schields
This charming folktale celebrates family through a mother cat, who tells her kittens about their Chinese ancestry.

***Alexander and the Terrible, Horrible,***
***No Good, Very Bad Day*** by Judith Viorst
Illustrated by Ray Cruz
Have you ever had "one of those days"? Poor Alexander experiences a series of humorous mishaps that make us realize things really aren't that bad after all!

***A Chair for My Mother***
Written and Illustrated by Vera B.Williams
After losing all their furniture in a fire, a young girl, her mother, and her grandmother save all their coins in a big glass jar. Working together, they are finally able to buy a big comfortable chair for their apartment.

# SUMMER ACTIVITIES AND PROJECTS

### Discovery Hike

Go on a "discovery hike." Examine interesting rocks, leaves, shells, and flowers. (Make sure plants are safe to touch!) Write down descriptions of the size, shape, and texture of the things you find.

### Fun at the Market

Go to the supermarket. Make lists of foods that start with certain letters, like carrots, corn, candles, cereal, and cream. Weigh vegetables and fruits on the scales to see how heavy they are. Talk about healthy and unhealthy foods with a parent or friend.

### Guess How Many!

Fill a jar with jellybeans or goldfish crackers. Try to guess how many items are in the jar. Ask your friends and family to guess. Then count the number of items to see who is closest. Challenge yourself by using different objects and different jars!

### Object Match-Up

Write the names of household objects on index cards, such as **couch**, **chair**, **fridge**, **bed**, **dresser**, **desk**, or **phone**. Read the index cards and tape them to the matching objects in your house.

### The Past and Today

Find out in what way things are different today than they were years ago. You can interview older relatives and friends. Ask questions about toys, cars, songs, appliances, movies, clothes, and family life. After the interviews, discuss how the world has changed over time.

### Photo Field Trip

Go to the zoo, park, museum, or another favorite place. Take lots of pictures. After the film is developed, make a scrapbook of the trip. Label the pictures and talk about the fun memories you made.

### A Recipe for Fun

Make a favorite traditional family recipe with your parents! Practice measuring with cups and spoons. Talk about where the recipe came from.

### Senses Walks

Take "senses walks" on warm summer days. Describe the sounds, smells, sights, and tastes as you walk with a parent or friend in different places. Compare what you experience with previous walks.

### Your Own Matching Game

Play a matching game using index cards. Match addition and subtraction facts, synonyms, antonyms, rhyming words, number words and numerals, and more!

# ANSWER KEY

**Page 6**

2. 2 **3** 4 5 6 **7**
 **8** 9 10 **11** 12
 Pattern : +1

3. 3 6 **9** 12 15 **18**
 21 **24** 27 **30**
 Pattern : +3

4. 5 **10** 15 20 **25**
 30 35 **40** 45
 Pattern : +5

**Page 7**

2. more
3. more
4. less
5. less
6. more

**Page 8**

1. 10
2. 8
3. 12
4. 12
5. 11
6. 10
7. 11
8. 15
9. 15
10. 8
11. 9
12. 9

1 and 6 are
 the same color.
2 and 10 are
 the same color.
3 and 4 are
 the same color.
5 and 7 are
 the same color.
8 and 9 are
 the same color.
11 and 12 are
 the same color.

**Page 9**

2 letters: or, to, he, me
3 letters: hoe, her, the,
 met, rot, hot
4 letters: more, home, tore.
 them, moth
5 letters: other
BIG word: mother

**Page 10**

2. tiny, yellow
3. large, noisy
4. short, curly, soft
5. long, shady
6. crisp, sweet

7. new, tasty
8. fun, warm
9. smart, funny
10. spicy, hot

**Page 11**

2. sh
3. sh
4. sh
5. ch
6. ch
7. ch
8. sh

**Page 12**

These pictures should
be colored:
girl brushing teeth
boy exercising
boy eating apple
girl washing hands

**Page 13**

Answers will vary.

**Page 14**

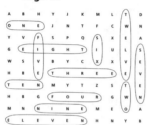

**Page 15**

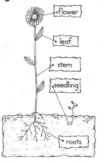

**Page 16**

**Page 17**

1. There are 16 verbs
 in the paragraph:
 got, has, barks, chases,
 walk, play, is, loves,
 showed, jump, catch,
 go, is, named, comes,
 call

 Answers to questions
 2–6 will vary.

**Page 18**

2. kitten
3. apple
4. baby
5. child
6. beach
7. milk
8. dinosaur
9. zoo
10. home

**Page 19**

**Page 20**

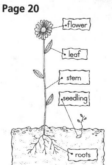

**Page 21**

**Page 22**

2. 1 5 9 13 **17 21 25**
 Pattern: +4

3. 14 12 **10** 8 **6 4** 2
 Pattern: -2

4. 3 6 9 **12** 15 **18 21**
 Pattern: +3

5. 10 9 8 **7 6** 5 4 **3**
 Pattern: -1

6. 10 15 20 **25** 30
 **35 40**
 Pattern: +5

**Page 23**

2. early
3. early
4. early
5. late
6. late

**Page 24**

2. pounds
3. ounces
4. ounces
5. pounds
6. pounds
7. pounds
8. ounces

**Page 25**

2. bell
3. wash
4. tax
5. jar
6. sky

**Page 26**

Today was a very windy
<u>day</u>! On my way to <u>school</u>,
my hat blew down the
street. My <u>hair</u> was a mess!
At school, I dropped my
notebook and <u>papers</u> went
flying everywhere. My best
<u>friend</u> Joshua helped me
catch them. When I got
home, a <u>branch</u> had blown
off of our tree. It <u>fell</u> in
the yard. When the <u>lights</u>
went out, we had to use
candles to see. It was fun
to eat <u>dinner</u> with candles.
Later, Dad told us a scary
<u>story</u>. Then, when I was in
<u>bed</u>, the wind <u>shook</u> the
windows. It was <u>spooky</u>!

**Page 27**

2. football
3. cupcake
4. starfish
5. sunshine
6. fireplace
7. doorbell
8. rainbow

**Page 28**

Ice is a solid.
Water is a liquid.
Steam is a gas.

2. solid
3. gas
4. solid
5. liquid
6. liquid
7. gas
8. solid
9. solid
10. liquid

**Page 29**

2. left
3. Elm Street
4. park
5. 3rd Avenue and
 Elm Street

**Page 30**

2. 3 inches
3. 4 inches
4. 3 inches
5. 3 $\frac{1}{2}$ inches

**Page 31**

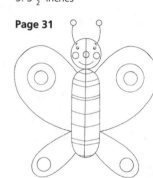

**Page 32**

These objects should
be circled:
2. soccer ball
3. trash can
4. gift

**Page 33**

2. bed, chair, dresser, table
3. breakfast, dinner,
 lunch, snack
4. book, desk, pencil,
 student
5. autumn, fall, summer,
 winter
6. beach, mall, park, zoo
7. crab, lobster,
 starfish, whale
8. goldfish, kitten,
 mouse, puppy

**Page 34**

2. It was a warm and breezy summer day.
3. My brother Carlos swam in the ocean.
4. I played in the sand and built a big sand castle.
5. Carlos and I hunted for shells along the seashore.
6. We found pink, white, and purple shells.
7. My dad made a big bonfire to cook dinner.
8. We ate hot dogs, chips, and crispy vegetables.
9. The ocean smelled fresh and salty.
10. Do you think we can come back next weekend?

**Page 35**

2. Mr.
3. Dr.
4. Jr.
5. Sr.
6. Ms.
7. Jan.
8. Feb.
9. Tues.
10. Thurs.
11. Aug.
12. Sun.
13. Sat.
14. Sept.
15. Dec.
16. Mon.
17. Oct.
18. Wed.
19. Fri.
20. Nov.
21. Apr.
22. Mar.

**Page 36**

These objects should be circled:
Winter: mittens, coat, boots, sweater, wool hat
Spring: T-shirt, dress, tank top, sandals, raincoat, shorts, skirt
Summer: tank top, shorts, sunglasses, sandals, T-shirt, dress
Fall: coat, jeans, gloves, sweater, scarf

**Page 37**

Continent: North America
Country: United States
State: Answers will vary.
City or Town:
    Answers will vary.
Street Address:
    Answers will vary.

**Page 38**

| | | | | | | | | | |
|---|---|---|---|---|---|---|---|---|---|
| 1 | 2 | 3 | 4 | 5 | 6 | 7 | 8 | 9 | 10 |
| 11 | 12 | 13 | 14 | 15 | 16 | 17 | 18 | 19 | 20 |
| 21 | 22 | 23 | 24 | 25 | 26 | 27 | 28 | 29 | 30 |
| 31 | 32 | 33 | 34 | 35 | 36 | 37 | 38 | 39 | 40 |
| 41 | 42 | 43 | 44 | 45 | 46 | 47 | 48 | 49 | 50 |
| 51 | 52 | 53 | 54 | 55 | 56 | 57 | 58 | 59 | 60 |
| 61 | 62 | 63 | 64 | 65 | 66 | 67 | 68 | 69 | 70 |
| 71 | 72 | 73 | 74 | 75 | 76 | 77 | 78 | 79 | 80 |
| 81 | 82 | 83 | 84 | 85 | 86 | 87 | 88 | 89 | 90 |
| 91 | 92 | 93 | 94 | 95 | 96 | 97 | 98 | 99 | 100 |

**Page 39**

2. 2 quarters, 4 dimes, 2 nickels
3. 3 quarters, 3 nickels, 1 dime
4. 3 quarters, 2 dimes, 1 nickel
5. 3 quarters, 2 dimes, 5 pennies

**Page 40**

**Page 41**

Would you like to come with me to the store? I am going to buy new school clothes. I would like to buy new shoes and a coat. After we shop, we can go out to lunch. Do you want burgers or pizza?

Mia and her friends were so excited! They were going to the zoo. At the zoo, they saw all kinds of wild animals. Which do you think was Mia's favorite? Of all the animals, Mia liked the giraffes the best.

Daniel was nervous. Today was the first game of the baseball playoffs. How many games had the Tigers won this season? Daniel was proud they had won all games but one. Oh no! It was starting to rain. They would have to wait until tomorrow to play.

**Page 42**

2. D
3. D
4. E
5. E
6. D
7. D
8. I
9. E
10. I

**Page 43**

1. 3, 1, 2, 4
2. 3, 4, 2, 1
3. 1, 3, 4, 2
4. 3, 1, 2, 4

**Page 44**

These pictures should be circled:
girl collecting cans
boy planting a tree
girl watering flowers

**Page 45**

2. bald eagle
3. Liberty Bell
4. flag
5. "The Star-Spangled Banner"
6. Capitol

**Page 46**

2. 40¢
3. $1.10
4. 75¢
5. $1.15

**Page 47**

2. 5
3. 1
4. 6

**Page 48**

2. $2 + 3 + 4 = 9$
3. $5 + 5 + 7 = 17$
4. $3 + 6 + 1 = 10$
5. $8 + 2 + 3 = 13$
6. $2 + 2 + 4 = 8$
7. $1 + 5 + 6 = 12$
8. $9 + 8 + 3 = 20$
9. $7 + 6 + 1 = 14$
10. $3 + 3 + 5 = 11$
11. $8 + 7 + 3 = 18$
12. $2 + 4 + 1 = 7$

**Page 49**

2. i
3. n
4. o
5. s
6. a
7. u
8. r
DINOSAUR

**Page 50**

2. ball, blank, book, brook
3. cave, clown, cold, creek
4. day, desk, dinner, drain
5. pail, people, plane, proud
6. raccoon, rhino, roam, rust
7. sale, slide, snake, story
8. team, tide, tool, trail

**Page 51**

1. last summer
2. the mountains
3. yellow flowers
4. a doe and her fawn
5. croaking, chirping

**Page 52**

Mammals: deer, monkey, skunk, lion
Reptiles: lizard, rattlesnake, alligator, dinosaur
Fish: catfish, tuna, trout, eel
Birds: chicken, robin, eagle, parrot

**Page 53**

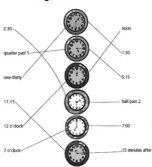

**Page 54**

2:30 — noon
quarter past 5 — 1:30
one-thirty — 5:15
11:15 — half past 2
12 o'clock — 7:00
7 o'clock — 15 minutes after 11

**Page 55**

2. 75¢
3. $1.50
4. $12
5. $15,000
6. $15
7. $5
8. $1

**Page 56**

2. sugar
3. 5
4. 4
5. peanut butter

**Page 57**

**Page 58**

2. o
3. o
4. t
5. s
6. t
7. e
8. p
9. s
FOOTSTEPS

**Page 59**

These balloons should be colored the same color:
happy / sad
quiet / loud
big / small
full / empty
sweet / sour
begin / end

**Page 60**

2. ship
3. bicycle
4. airplane
5. helicopter
6. hot air balloon
7. motorcycle
8. sailboat
9. scooter
10. train
11. truck
12. skateboard

**Page 61**

Land: car, bicycle, motorcycle, scooter, train, truck, skateboard
Air: airplane, helicopter, hot air balloon
Water: sailboat, ship

**Page 62**

2. pink
3. purple
4. orange
5. gray
6. Answers will vary.

**Page 63**

2. 2 tens, 1 one
3. 4 tens, 2 ones
4. 1 ten, 5 ones
5. 3 tens, 6 ones
6. 5 tens, 0 ones

**Page 64**

2.

Each piece = $\frac{1}{2}$

3.

Each piece = $\frac{1}{2}$

4.

Each piece = $\frac{1}{4}$

5.

Each piece = $\frac{1}{2}$

6.

Each piece = $\frac{1}{4}$

**Page 65**

2. thermometer
3. ruler
4. ruler
5. scale
6. measuring cup
7. thermometer
8. scale

**Page 66**

1. 1, 5, 2, 3, 4; spaghetti
2. 5, 4, 3, 1, 2;
   brushed my teeth
3. 4, 2, 5, 1, 3;
   toast with jam

**Page 67**

**Page 68**

2. marsupials
3. pouches
4. joey
5. 10 months

**Page 69**

1, Egg; 2, Caterpillar;
3, Pupa; 4, Butterfly

**Page 70**

2. teacher
3. mail carrier
4. veterinarian
5. doctor
6. clerk
7. bus driver
8. dentist
9. nurse
10. police officer

**Page 71**

**Page 72**

2. afternoon
3. morning
4. morning
5. night
6. afternoon
7. night
8. night

**Page 73**

2. yes
3. no
4. no
5. yes
6. no

**Page 74**

2. d
3. c
4. a
5. b

**Page 75**

2. koala
3. giraffe
4. rhino
5. tiger
6. zebra
7. snake
8. elephant
9. panda
10. lion
11. monkey
12. hippo
Bonus Word: alligator

**Page 76**

Answers will vary.

**Page 77**

2. vet
3. water
4. walks
5. food
6. play
7. love

**Page 78**

Answers will vary.

**Page 79**

Row 1: MONKEY
Row 2: TURKEY
Row 3: DONKEY

**Page 80**

**Page 81**

2. 29 **30** 31
3. 54 55 **56**
4. 16 **17 18** 19
5. 48 **49** 50 **51**
6. 32 33 **34 35**
7. 96 **97** 98 **99 100**
8. 61 62 **63 64 65**
10. 91 90 **89**
11. 20 **19** 18
12. 72 71 **70 69**
13. 80 **79 78** 77
14. 57 **56** 55 **54**
15. 29 **28 27** 26 **25**
16. 44 **43** 42 **41 40**

**Page 82**

Top of egg: cub, fog, grab,
   shell, hid
Bottom of egg: tune, cone,
   mail, neat, lime
SNAKE

**Page 83**

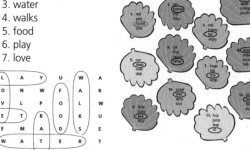

**Page 84**

2. buck, 1
3. roost / er, 2
4. wheat, 1
5. No / vem / ber, 3
6. Sat / ur / day, 3
7. per / son, 2
8. in / stead, 2
9. my / self, 2
10. un / der / stand, 3
11. pub / lic, 2
12. bull / doz / er, 3

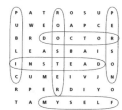

**Page 85**

These objects
should be circled:
   grapes, bread, steak,
   chicken, lettuce, yogurt,
   cheese, carrots, cereal

These objects should
be crossed out:
   candy bar, cake,
   French fries

**Page 86**

Answers will vary.

**Page 87**

Answers will vary.

**Page 88**

2. 1 ten, 5 ones = 15
3. 2 tens, 0 ones = 20
4. 1 ten, 9 ones = 19
5. 2 tens, 6 ones = 26
6. 3 tens, 1 one = 31

**Page 89**

2. song
3. trees
4. care
The poem at the bottom
should have a rhyming
word pair.

**Page 90**

The written letter will vary.

**Page 91**

These objects
should be colored:
   feather, leaf, twig,
   crayon, flower

These objects should
be crossed out:
   penny, rock,
   paper clip, key